Icons

Reading Sacred Images

by
Fr John Baggley

*All booklets are published thanks to the
generous support of the members of the
Catholic Truth Society*

CATHOLIC TRUTH SOCIETY
PUBLISHERS TO THE HOLY SEE

Contents

Introduction 3

What's in a Word? 7

Why Holy Icons? 12

The Anonymous Iconographers 17

The First Named Iconographers 22

Evolution of the Holy Icons 27

The Language of the Holy Icons 30

What do we discover through the Holy Icons? 35

Where do we see the Holy Icons? 39

Commentary on Plates 47

   1. Portrait of a Bearded Young Man 47

   2. The Annunciation 48

   3. The Nativity of Christ 53

   4. The Mother of God, Hodegitria 57

   5. The icon of the Mother of God, Eleousa 60

   6. The Mother of God of the Sign 64

   7. Christ the Saviour 66

   8. The Transfiguration of Christ 68

   9. Anastasis - Resurrection 71

   10. St Sergius of Radonezh (c.1314-1392) 76

   11. The Holy Trinity Icon of Andrei Rublev 80

Living and Praying with the Holy Icons 85

Abbreviations 90

Futher reading 91

Introduction

Icons have been part of the prayer life of the Church for about seventeen hundred years. For many centuries they were the main form of Christian liturgical art. In the Eastern Churches they continue to have the same dominant liturgical significance, even though styles have varied in different times and places. In the Western Church icons have never completely disappeared, but they have been overshadowed by other forms of sacred art with a more naturalistic style, and the rich tradition of Christian sculpture. Some icons are to be found in Rome and Venice, together with Ravenna, and Monreale and Cefalu in Sicily where the Byzantine world met with the Western world.

During the 16th and 17th centuries the Catholic Church sought to renew sacred art in the Church. The Council of Trent re-affirmed the rightful place of images in Catholic worship and devotion, using the same theology which had been articulated some eight hundred years earlier during the Iconoclast Controversy: "The images of Christ, of the Virgin Mother of God, and of other saints must be kept and preserved in churches; proper honour and devotion should be paid to them, not because there is any divinity or power in them for which they must be venerated, or because one should ask something of them or put faith in the images, as once the pagans did, putting their hope in idols, but because the honour given to them is to be referred to the prototype which they represent; through images, therefore, we adore Christ and venerate the saints whose likeness they manifest. This has been ordained by decrees of Councils - especially the Second Council of Nicea - against the opponents of icons".

Images in Vatican II

The Church again affirmed the place of sacred art in its worship at the Second Vatican Council, emphasising the diverse possibilities which are opened up with the different peoples and cultures embraced within the Church (sometimes leading to an artistic individualism that would be rejected by the Orthodox Churches). "Very rightly the fine arts are considered to rank among the noblest activities of man's genius, and this applies especially to religious art and to its highest achievement, which is sacred art. These arts, by their very nature, are oriented toward the infinite beauty of God which they attempt in some way to portray by the work of human hands; they achieve their purpose of redounding to God's praise and glory in proportion as they are directed the more exclusively to the single aim of turning men's minds devoutly toward God. Holy Mother Church has therefore always been the friend of the fine arts and has ever sought their noble help, with the special aim that all things set apart for use in divine worship should be truly worthy, becoming, and beautiful, signs and symbols of the supernatural world, and for this purpose she has trained artists. In fact, the Church has, with good reason, always reserved to herself the right to pass judgment upon the arts, deciding which of the works of artists are in accordance with faith, piety, and cherished traditional laws, and thereby fitted for sacred use". ... "The practice of placing sacred images in churches so that they may be venerated by the faithful is to be maintained" (*Sacrosanctum Concilium*, 122 & 125).

The forty years since the Second Vatican Council coincide with a period in which the use of icons by Western Christians has increased enormously. Reasons for this include developments in the study, conservation and creation of icons, greater opportunities for travel, the dispersion of many Orthodox Christians around the world, and ecumenical contacts which have been promoted since Vatican II. The increased use of icons has been warmly welcomed and also greeted with caution in Catholic circles. The caution stems from an awareness of the danger of 'fads and fashions' in spiritual matters, and of the complexities involved in adapting devotional traditions from a different culture, albeit a profoundly Christian one. The welcome witnesses to the spiritual significance and beauty of icons, which resist the cult of originality and individuality which has dominated much modern Christian art.

The presence of God

With all visual sacred art there is an interaction between the viewer and the work of art. We use our eyes to behold and see. If the art is sculptural, we may walk round it, examine it in detail, or stand back for a different view. Michelangelo's *David* is brilliantly situated for it to be seen from all possible angles, and the same is true of Rodin's *The Burghers of Calais*: it is almost impossible not to walk round sculptures like these. With icons, things are different: we cannot walk around an icon. The icon faces us, and many people discover a greater sense of 'presence' in the two dimensional icon than in sculptures that we instinctively want to touch and scrutinize. The icon has the capacity to encourage us to stand still, to look, to pray, to 'be present' with what is set before us, be it an image of Christ, the Mother of God, the saints, or events in the life of Christ.

I hope this booklet will help you to know something about the theology and history of icons, but above all to use them in your praying. Some people 'click' with icons very quickly; for others their appreciation takes longer to mature; some people find them alien and difficult. If you find that icons do 'speak' to you, you may want to go further in your exploration of this form of sacred art. Suggestions for further reading and places to visit are given in the booklet.

What's in a Word?

In English the word *icon* can be used as a general term for an image. It is often used in connection with religious imagery, and the term *iconography* can relate to any consistent scheme of imagery, religious or secular. However, two modern secular applications of the word *icon* have gained wide currency. First, in the world of fashion and entertainment, people can be described as *icons* if they epitomize certain trends in style or culture. Second, in the world of computers and electronic technology certain images on the screen are known as *icons*. Click on the icon and you enter a whole new world of information and imagery. The icon in electronic technology opens up vast prospects which seem out of all proportion to the tiny image on the screen. This modern usage of the word icon has interesting parallels with the theological use of the term - but we will come on to that later.

At the very beginning of the Bible, we read that human beings are made to be in the image and likeness of God: "God said, 'Let us make man in our image, after our likeness; and let them have dominion over the fish of the sea, and over the birds of the air, and over the cattle, and over all the earth, and over every creeping thing that creeps upon the earth.' So God created man in his own image, in the image of God he created him; male and female he created them. And God blessed them, and God said to them, 'Be fruitful and multiply, and fill the earth and subdue it; and have dominion over the fish of the sea and over the birds of the air and over every living thing that moves upon the earth.' ... And it was so. And God saw everything that he had made, and behold, it was very good" (cf. *Gn* 1:26-31, 5:1-2, 9:6).

Representing God

Human beings are to represent God within his creation, to be present within the created order blessed with an intimate relationship with the Creator, to share God's authority and creativity. Throughout history, statues and images of kings, emperors, dictators, presidents and others in authority express the reality and extent of their power. For the ancient Israelites, when foreign conquerors erected their images in Jerusalem and in the Temple, this was an affront to God and the Promised Land he had given to his people. The presence of foreign images in holy places was an act of sacrilege and desecration. Similarly when human life and behaviour falls short of the glory of God, the image of God is disfigured; humans embody and become images of that which is distorted and evil.

In the second century BC when Jewish scholars translated their scriptures into Greek, the word they used for *image* in the book of Genesis was *eikon*, from which we derive the word *icon*. We are created to be *icons* of God! That is our human vocation. At the time of Christ, the Roman emperor's *eikon* on the coinage was a visible sign of his rule and authority (cf. *Mt* 22:20). In the Roman law courts, the imperial icons showed that justice was being administered on the authority of the Emperor. The late 6th century Rossano Gospel has two illustrations of Christ before Pilate. On the table before Pilate are two imperial images, while behind Pilate stand two attendants with poles supporting imperial icons. The nature of Pilate's authority could not be stated more clearly.

He is the image of the invisible God

The following quotation with the word *icon* should be regarded as a 'foundation text' for our understanding. In the letter to the Colossians St Paul says: "May you be strengthened with all power, according to his glorious might, for all endurance and patience with joy, giving thanks to the Father, who has qualified us to share in the inheritance of the saints in light. He has delivered us from the dominion of darkness and transferred us to the kingdom of his beloved Son, in whom we have redemption, the forgiveness of sins. **He is the image (*eikon*) of the invisible God**, the first-born of all creation;

for in him all things were created, in heaven and on earth, visible and invisible, whether thrones or dominions or principalities or authorities - all things were created through him and for him. He is before all things, and in him all things hold together. He is the head of the body, the church; he is the beginning, the first-born from the dead, that in everything he might be pre-eminent. For in him all the fullness of God was pleased to dwell, and through him to reconcile to himself all things, whether on earth or in heaven, making peace by the blood of his cross" (*Col* 1:11-20). St Paul is caught up in a great act of prayer and praise arising from his life in Christ, giving thanks for all that he has received through Christ. Then he simply states that Jesus Christ is the *eikon* of the invisible God. He brings together the role of Christ in creation, redemption, and the life we share in the Church. We are created to be icons of God. Jesus Christ *is* the icon of the invisible God. Christian understanding of human life develops in the light of the creation story where Adam and Eve are created to be icons of God, in the light of the story of sin and turning away from God, and in the light of the story of our redemption, where Jesus Christ is revealed as the true icon of the invisible God. God made manifest in the humanity of Jesus enables fallen humanity to be restored to the true image and likeness of God, and to full communion with the Holy Trinity. This is the background against which we can appreciate the Church's holy icons.

Image and likeness

Something should be said about the combined use of the words *image* and *likeness*. In the Byzantine, Russian and Greek traditions of theology a distinction is made between the fundamental given-ness of the image of God, and the likeness of God which is acquired through repentance, grace and a life lived in accordance with the Gospel. A few quotations will illustrate this perspective. "All men are made in God's image, but to be in his likeness is granted only to those who through great love have brought their own freedom into subjection to God. For only when we do not belong to ourselves do we become like him who through love has reconciled us to himself". (St Diodochus of Photiki c. 400 - c. 486. *Phil*. I, p. 253)

"God is love and the source of love: the Creator of all things has endowed us with this characteristic of love. Where love is missing all the elements of the imagery are deformed". (St Gregory of Nyssa c. 330-395). "In the Bible the image of God is distinguished from his likeness, and Church tradition has long ago explained that by image is signified the actual, ontological gift of a personal spiritual foundation, conferred by God on every man as such. Likeness, instead, signifies the virtuality of perfect spiritual grace, the power given to the empirical person of conforming his whole being to the divine image - i.e. of incarnating, in so far as possible, the image of God ... in life and in personality" (Fr Pavel Florenskii 1882 - 1937).

Why Holy Icons?

Human beings have a great capacity for sense perception. We see, hear, smell, taste, touch and handle different elements in the external world. Through our senses we communicate with each other and discover our place in the wider world. In the last hundred years we have been increasingly exposed to visual stimuli through film, television, the internet and advertising media, but for thousands of years different civilizations have used painting, mosaics and sculpture - the visual arts - to express their values and ideals. Sacred and secular art has a long history, and this is certainly true of Mediterranean and Middle-Eastern cultures. Excavations at Pompeii have revealed many wall paintings in both domestic and public buildings. Egyptian, Greek and Roman paintings and sculpture were used to express political and religious beliefs. Many of these would have been viewed with deep suspicion by people in the Jewish and early Christian tradition. The early Christians were not likely to adopt the art that was commonly used to depict the Roman emperors or the Greek gods. Much secular or pagan imagery had the wrong associations for Christian artists wanting to express their faith in Christ.

Origins

To see the origins of the holy icons we need to look at two of the earliest traditions of Christian art. First, the art which has survived in the catacombs, the places of early Christian burials in Rome. This is not public art in the sense that the Church's art became public after it gained freedom of worship early in the fourth century. Catacomb art is associated with the burial of members of the often persecuted minority Christian community, and it expresses the faith in which the bodies of the faithful departed have been laid to rest. Images from the Old Testament include Adam and Eve, Jonah, Daniel, and Jacob's ladder. From the New Testament we have Christ and the Mother of God, the Last Supper, the multiplication of the loaves and fishes, Christ with the Apostles, the woman with the issue of blood and the raising of Lazarus. Two themes which do have connections with the non-Christian art are the Orant and the Good Shepherd. The *Orant* (or *Orans*) is a standing figure with arms raised in prayer, symbolizing piety in the Roman world. This is adopted into the Christian "vocabulary" of images which depict the faithful departed. It also becomes a major type of image of the Mother of God. Similarly the image of a shepherd with a sheep on his shoulders symbolized philanthropy, love for humanity. For Christians this image conveyed the truth of

Christ the Good Shepherd, with all the resonances which that image has in Old and New Testament about God as the Shepherd of his people. In catacomb art we see the depiction of Biblical texts at an early stage of development. Some of these images gain a permanent place in the Church's visual language.

Portraiture

Second, there is the art which develops from a tradition of funeral art in Egypt. Mummy portraits or *Fayyum* portraits are a group of about 700 panel portraits which have been discovered near the oasis of El Fayyum, about 100 miles south of Cairo. Very few of these were known before the late 19th century. They derive from the Hellenistic culture of Roman Egypt between the first and fourth centuries AD. These panel portraits were made during the lifetime of their subjects, and then placed over the face at the time of burial. The paintings are generally on wooden boards, but sometimes on linen, using the wax encaustic technique where the pigments are mixed in hot wax and applied to the panel with a spatula. Many of these portraits convey an intense sense of the individuality of the person, a living being whose spiritual identity has not ended with death and burial. The faces, and particularly the eyes, have a remarkable intensity, expressing far more than physical resemblance. There is a sense of presence, of a profound humanity, a combination of sorrow and beauty. This tradition of portraiture had an eloquence which was able to serve the Christian Church and communicate its message (cf. plate 1). It is from this background and techniques that the tradition of the holy icons begins. The earliest surviving panel icons date from the 6th century; some can be seen in Rome, others at the Monastery of St Katherine at the foot of Mount Sinai, and a few others in museums around the world.

Why holy?

Why *holy* icons? Because Christians needed an imagery which would express what they believed about the Holy God who had been revealed in Jesus Christ, the Holy One of God (cf. *Jn* 6:69), and also express what they wished to commemorate in connection with the holy ones of their communities who had lived and died for the faith. The presence of icons in churches for the Divine Liturgy reinforces the sense of the presence of Christ and his holy ones in the Communion of Saints. The holy icons of the Church counteract profane and political imagery, and complement the verbal imagery of Scripture and Liturgy. "Hearing is equal to sight, and it is necessary to use both senses", wrote St Theodore of Studium (759-826). This truth is also expressed in an Orthodox tradition that St Luke was the first iconographer: after Pentecost the Holy Spirit worked not only through the writings of St Luke in his Gospel and the Acts of the Apostles, but through his painting of icons of the Mother of God with her Son. The Spirit, the Word and the Icon work together to restore our lives as true icons of God. Another tradition precious to Orthodox Christians concerns the *acheiropoietos icon*, literally *the icon not made by human hands*: Agbar king of Edessa sent messengers to Christ asking him to come and heal him; instead of returning with the envoys Christ placed a cloth on his own face which received his image, and this was sent to Agbar, who was healed when he beheld the face of Christ. From this tradition we have the image of the Holy Face which can be seen in most Orthodox churches. It is an image which reinforces the truth of St Paul's statement: "It is the God who said, 'Let light shine out of darkness', who has shone in our hearts to give the light of the knowledge of the glory of God in the face of Christ" (2 *Co* 4:6).

The Anonymous Iconographers

The earliest icons were painted by the same artists who produced the Fayyum portraits - ordinary anonymous artists engaged in portraiture, and who made images for the Christian churches and homes. Later on, work was done by more specialized artists, in many instances linked to monastic communities. The names of the artists are not known. Not until the 14th century do we begin to know the names of iconographers. In the 4th century people like St Basil and St Gregory of Nyssa took the presence of Christian imagery for granted. St Gregory commented that "the silent painting speaks on the walls and does much good", and St Basil articulated the distinction between the veneration of an image and the honouring of the 'prototype' who is represented in the image. By the 6th century panel icons, mosaics and wall paintings were a normal feature of Church life. Icons would be found in houses and workshops as well as in churches. St Bede tells us of the meeting of St Augustine and his companions with Ethelbert, king of Kent in 597: the monks "approached the king carrying a silver cross as their standard, and the likeness of our Lord and Saviour painted on a board". The scene is illustrated in the Chapel of St Gregory the Great in Westminster Cathedral. Later

St Benedict Biscop (c. 628-89) went through Europe seeking devotional items for his monastery at Wearmouth and Jarrow, and icons were among the holy objects he brought back from Rome.

Early controversy

In the West we are familiar with the conflicts over religious imagery which raged through Europe in the 16th century, and again in England in the 17th century. We may be familiar with contemporary Christian groups and followers of Islam which oppose religious images, but the earliest serious Christian conflict over such issues began in the 8th century. Some within the Church had reservations about the widespread presence and veneration of icons; when the Islamic armies, with their strong anti-iconic and anti-Trinitarian theology, were successful against the Christian Byzantine forces, some began to think that the Muslims might not be mistaken in these matters. The bitter 'Iconoclast Controversy' was sparked off by Imperial decrees calling for the removal of some icons, and it spread throughout the Byzantine world from 726 to 843, with a period when the defenders of the holy icons were in the ascendant from 787 to 815. The *iconoclasts* sought to destroy the holy icons; the *iconophiles* or *iconodules* defended the icons and the practice of venerating them. Thousands of icons were destroyed during this conflict, and many iconodules were martyred for their faith.

Images and the Incarnation

The defenders of the icons believed the iconoclasts were not simply attacking Church art, but the reality of the Incarnation, and its implications for Christian faith and worship. The commandment given to Moses that prohibited the making and worshipping of graven images was given before the Incarnation took place, "before the age of grace... when God had not yet been revealed in the flesh" (St Theodore of Studium). The fact that "the Word became flesh and dwelt among us, full of grace and truth" (*Jn* 1:14) changes the whole situation: God has been manifested in the flesh; the God-Man Jesus Christ is "the image of the invisible God" (*Col* 1:15). The invisible God has been made manifest, has been seen, touched and handled (1 *Jn* 1:1-3) in the person of Jesus Christ. To represent the person of Christ in icons is not idolatry; it is to affirm that revelation can be perceived through the eye as well as through the ear. For St Theodore and the iconophiles seeing is of vital importance. "If merely mental contemplation were sufficient, it would have been sufficient for Him to come to us in a merely mental way." Christ "nowhere told anyone to write down the 'concise word'; yet his image was drawn in writing by the apostles and has been preserved up to the present. Whatever is marked there with paper and ink, the same is marked on the icon with various pigments or some other material.

For the great Basil says: 'Whatever the words of the narrative offer, the picture silently shows by imitation'". The titles of two of the major works from the iconodule writers are significant: *On the Holy Icons* by St Theodore the Studite, and *On the Divine Images* by St John of Damascus. It is *holy* icons and *divine* images which are being defended, not religious art in general. The Seventh Ecumenical Council at Nicea in 787 (Nicea II) articulated the theology of the icon. It stressed the ecclesial nature of iconography: "Iconography was not at all invented by the painters, but on the contrary, it is an approved institution and a tradition of the Catholic Church". The nature of the veneration of the sacred images was clarified: true adoration (*latreia*) is given to God alone; honour or veneration (*proskynesis*) is given through the material image to whoever is represented therein. The decisions of 787 were re-affirmed when the controversy ended with the Triumph of Orthodoxy in 843.

Pope John Paul II's encyclical *Duodecimum Saeculum* (1987) to mark the 1200th anniversary of the Second Council of Nicea reiterates the centrality of Christ for our appreciation of the holy icons: "The iconography of Christ involves the whole faith in the reality of the Incarnation and its inexhaustible meaning for the Church and the world. If the Church practises it, it is because she is convinced that the God revealed in Jesus Christ has truly redeemed and sanctified the flesh and the whole sensible world, that is man with his five senses, to allow him to be ever renewed in the image of his creator" (cf. *Col* 3:10).

John Paul II draws attention to the range of Christian imagery envisaged by the Council: "Nicaea II sanctioned the tradition according to which 'venerable and holy images, done in colour, mosaics and all other appropriate materials, of our Lord God and Saviour Jesus Christ as well as those of Mary Immaculate, the Holy Theotokos, the honourable angels and all holy and pious people are to be exposed in the holy churches of God, on sacred vessels and vestments, on the walls and on the floors, in the houses and in the streets'." He also stresses the twin senses of seeing and hearing: "Just as the reading of material books allows the hearing of the living word of the Lord, so also the showing of the painted icon allows those who contemplate it to accede to the mystery of salvation by the sense of sight".

The First Named Iconographers

The Triumph of Orthodoxy in 843 ensured a significant place for icons in the Church, but the developments were different in East and West. In the West there were no martyrs during the iconoclast controversy; the issues involved had not been faced with the same intensity as in the East. Some of the subtleties of the debate were not appreciated in the West, where the use of imagery and illustrations in churches was largely defended on the principle of 'the poor man's Bible': what the unlettered and ignorant were unable to learn through the written word could be assimilated through illustrations in churches. The theology of the image and its prototype, and the issue of the veneration of images simply did not have the same significance in the West as in the East, where the controversy was part of a continuing defence of Orthodoxy against heresy. Leaders like Charlemagne were unable to appreciate the theological issues that were involved, and were reluctant to go along with the full theological defence adopted in 787, even though these had been wholeheartedly affirmed by Pope Hadrian I.

In the centuries that followed the Triumph of Orthodoxy, military, political and linguistic issues strained communications between East and West. In the East a dynamic development of iconography took place after 843. There was an urgent need to replace images that had been destroyed, a renewed zeal for devotion to the holy icons that was the fruit of martyrdom, and a desire to expand the repertoire of images. Nicaea II had permanently linked the work of the iconographers to the doctrine and liturgy of the Church. Icons could not gain a place in public worship and liturgy until they had been 'received' and blessed by a bishop or priest. It was clear that iconographers worked as servants of Christ, of the Church and of the Faith it professes. Just as copyists who reproduced the manuscripts of the Bible had to be faithful to the received text, so the iconographer has to be faithful to the faith and theology of the Church. He or she is 'writing' icons to communicate the faith. As Pope John Paul says: "Art for art's sake, which only refers to the author, without establishing a relationship with the divine world, does not have its place in the Christian concept of the icon".

Depicting the Death and Resurrection of Christ

From the 9th century onwards we see images of the Crucifixion with a dead Christ (a major change from Christ on the Cross 'reigning from the tree', clothed and alive). Reticence about depicting the dead Christ seemed to be overcome. From the same period we find examples of the *Anastasis*, the image which becomes the chief representation of the Resurrection in Orthodox Church art. Christ is shown raising Adam and Eve from the depths of Hades and bringing them up with him into glory (cf. plate 9). This imagery develops from homilies which had explored the cosmic significance of Christ's death, descent and resurrection, as well as from specific Biblical texts (cf. *Ac* 2:22-36; 1 *P* 3:18-19). In 12th century Constantinople some monastic communities became increasingly interested in the place of the Mother of God in the Passion of Christ. Their liturgical poetry explores the sorrow of the Virgin as she finds Simeon's prophecy (*Lk* 2:35) fulfilled while she stands at the foot of the Cross. This liturgical material finds expression in images of the Deposition, where the Mother of God holds the dead Christ, and in other images where the dead Christ and his grieving Mother are juxtaposed. Likewise this exploration of sorrow and suffering finds expression in icons of the Mother of God (cf. plate 5), and also in Western devotional images after Crusaders and traders brought back such icons from their campaigns in the East.

As missions took the faith into Russia and the Balkans the creation of icons took place in different cultures. Constantinople remained the spiritual, cultural and theological nerve centre of the Orthodox Churches until its conquest by the Ottoman Turks in 1453. By that time many of the artistic and spiritual traditions of Orthodoxy had taken root in Russia and the Balkans and developed with a new vitality. From this period some prominent names begin to appear in connection with icons. Theophanes the Greek worked in Constantinople, then in Novgorod, Moscow and other Russian cities in the late 14th and early 15th centuries. His work influenced Andrei Rublev and Daniel Chorny, and later, Dionysii (1450 - 1508) and his school; these were all involved in decorating Russian churches, commissioned by princes, bishops, monasteries or guilds. Some were monks, and many icons were produced in monastic workshops by both monks and lay workers. The network of monastic links between Mount Athos and Russian monasteries continued to nurture the spiritual and artistic life of Russia.

Monasticism

After the fall of Constantinople the life of Christians in the Greek speaking world was greatly constrained. The glory days of Byzantium were over, but the heritage was not completely lost. Monastic centres at St Katherine's in Sinai, Mount Athos, Patmos and the Meteora maintained a spiritual and artistic vitality under Turkish rule. Crete and Cyprus became major centres of Orthodox life where the iconographic traditions were sustained, and trade links with Venice led to an interaction of stylistic influences between Orthodox and Catholic communities. In the 15th and 16th centuries well known iconographers from the Cretan and Cypriot background include Andreas and Nikolaos Ritzos, Michael Damaskinos, and Domenikos Theotokopoulos who is better known in the West as El Greco. A signature on an icon is generally accompanied by the phrase, 'By the hand of ....', showing that the artist is the servant through whom the icon has come into existence.

The great tradition of Orthodox iconography suffered corrosive Western influence in the aftermath of the collapse of the Byzantine Empire. In the Mediterranean world Orthodox artists became increasingly familiar with Western art and a blending of traditions took place, sometimes encouraged by patrons who wanted Western style images. In 18th century Russia Tsar Peter the Great was determined to spread the Western styles to which he became attracted through his visits to European cities. The palaces and churches of his new city St Petersburg were markedly different from traditional Russian and Orthodox buildings, and their decoration was influenced by Renaissance art. Peter's 'crusade' to adopt European culture led to changes in iconography, with new images looking more like Western paintings. Some traditional iconography did survive, particularly in the marginalized communities of the Old Believers who rejected reforms introduced in 1666.

Evolution of the Holy Icons

Churches are not always dry, clean and warm places. Dirt, damp and decay have left their marks. Even in a dry climate dust, smoke from candles and incense, and the effects of human presence have created an atmosphere in which the pristine surface of a new icon is destined to become discoloured and darkened as the varnish gradually attracts a layer of dirt. What was originally clearly visible became less distinct and sometimes completely invisible. A solution to this problem was to re-paint the icon. Over the centuries icons could be re-painted or recreated many times. The style of later re-painting could differ from the original, and by the time styles had been influenced by Western art, the differences could be dramatic. Sometimes a board would be re-shaped and used again for a different image. The addition of a metal cover known as an *oklad* or *riza* changed the visual impact of an icon. Such covers protected the surface of the icon from human contact when it was venerated and were often ornate, with jewellery or devotional objects attached as thank-offerings. An icon created in the 10th or 13th century, for example, could look very different by the end of the 19th century.

Restoring Icons

Towards the end of the 19th century the cleaning and restoration of icons began to take place in Russia. Layers of dirt and over-painting were removed in the search for the original image. Sometimes images were damaged in the process. Familiar icons such as the Vladimir Mother of God (early 12th century) and Andrei Rublev's Holy Trinity (early 15th century) looked very different before restoration work revealed the glory and wonder of what lay beneath the later accretions. These developments prompted the Russian nobleman Prince Evgenii Trubetskoi (1863-1920) to write his collection of essays *Icons: Theology in Colour* (1915-1917). One of the key points which Trubetskoi made was that icons were meant to be seen. That is a statement of the obvious, but it was not at all obvious to people who were familiar with dark holy objects covered with a metal oklad. The holy object was venerated and used as a focal point for prayer and devotion, but the image was often invisible or unrecognizable. Trubetskoi made the point that the icon had become a sort of talismanic object, something holy and credited with spiritual power and significance - but not used in ways that were in keeping with the theology of the icon articulated during the Iconoclast Controversy. The theology stated at Nicea in 787 only made sense if the image was visible and recognizable.

The restoration work which began in the late 19th century has enabled us to see what was created during some of the great periods of spiritual and artistic accomplishment in the Church's history. The theological insights of people like Trubetskoi have been a major stimulus to the revival of interest in icons and their spiritual significance. A third significant factor for developments during the last 90 years has been the Russian diaspora following from the Revolution of 1917. Russian exiles settling in many parts of the world preserved their faith and built churches for their communities; even though faced with great poverty iconographers created the images which were needed for the churches. From Paris the influence of Leonid Ouspensky and Gregory Kroug has been widespread. In the Greek world people like Constantine Cavarnos and Photios Kontaglou have been influential. During the Communist period in Russia interest in iconography was sustained through the State icon restoration workshops as well as within the Church. Since the collapse of the Soviet Union in 1991, the freedom granted to the Russian Orthodox Church has led to a burgeoning of iconography as new churches have been built and decorated with frescoes and icons.

The Language of the Holy Icons

Our first encounter with icons may not be easy, for they are seriously different from many of our assumptions about art and imagery. We are familiar with realistic images in photography and Western religious art, but icons are different: they are a non-naturalistic form of art; they are not trying to convey a 'realistic' picture of a person or a scene. The intention behind the icon is to make the invisible visible - to put us in touch with something that is greater than the sum of the visible elements, to put us in touch with a different kind of 'reality', to raise us up to the divine realm. To achieve these goals iconographers work with various conventions, symbolic images and styles which constitute part of the language of the holy icons. Other elements come from the Biblical or liturgical texts which have helped to shape the images. If we look at almost any part of the Bible we find that much of the language involves metaphor, symbolism and verbal imagery, all of which have echoes or resonances in other parts of Sacred Scripture and the Liturgy of the Church.

Features and gestures

Looking at icons of Christ, the Mother of God and the saints we realize that the central figure is positioned in the icon in a way that establishes a relationship with the person who stands before it. We often become aware of a strong sense of gesture and direction in an icon. Hands direct our attention. The eyes often have an enigmatic quality, looking at us, but also beyond us, enfolding us in a gaze which seems to be linked to another world (cf. plates 4, 6, 7, 10).

The person we behold in an icon often has enlarged ears, deep set eyes, a rather long nose, and a closed mouth. These conventions convey a powerful sense of inner attentiveness, listening, seeing, stillness - so different from our noisy 'driven' behaviour when we lose the ability to listen, to see and to be attentive. Sometimes icons can slow us down, and help us to be still. They have the power to put us in touch with a whole spiritual tradition of inner prayer, prayer of the heart, where heart and soul are purified and renewed by the grace of the Holy Spirit.

Labels

An icon should be recognizable, and the name is there to remove any doubt. Christ's halo is marked with the Cross, the name Jesus Christ is placed near the figure of Christ, and the halo is inscribed with letters indicating 'The One', the 'I am that I am', who made himself known to Moses through the Burning Bush (*Ex* 3:14). Thus the icon of the incarnate Son is able to convey the truth of both his humanity and his divinity (cf. plate 7). Similarly with icons of the Mother of God, she is always referred to as such, with either the full title or an abbreviated form on the icon. This links her inextricably with the Incarnation. The three illustrations in plates 4, 5 and 6 show three different types of Mother of God icons, but many other types also exist.

Perspective

We are familiar with scenes where the 'lines' of perspective converge at the back of a picture, and figures there are smaller than those at the front. In icons we generally find an inverse form of perspective, where the lines converge in front of the icon, with the effect of projecting the image towards us. This can reinforce the sense that I am the one who is being addressed through the icon (cf. plate 11). Another detail which helps to hold our attention is *axial symmetry*, the use of a strong central vertical line around which the image is created (cf. plates 6, 7, 8, 10, 11).Circular and triangular forms are also used (cf. plates 8, 11). These compositional features are not slavishly followed, but are part of the structure of an icon within which the central people or events are presented to us. Perhaps the most noticeably non-naturalistic details can be seen in architectural features (cf. plate 2). Some of these seem to have more in common with the world of dreams rather than any known tradition of architecture. Often parts of buildings simply do not join up properly, arches start on a wall and end in space, roof details may be similarly unrealistic, and there may be a whole variety of 'perspectives'. These strange details seem to create an awareness of the extra-ordinary nature of what is being set before us, and that it is being seen from a divine perspective.

Backgrounds

In some icons for the Church Feasts we find a variety of episodes brought together in the one icon. Most people in icons are shown 'full face'. Even if the head is slightly turned, both eyes are visible. People of lesser significance in the story, or people of sinister intent, are often shown with only one side of the face visible, such as the midwives and the sinister shepherd figure in the Nativity icon (cf. plate 3). Events shown on a mountain or against a mountainous background remind us that in the Bible mountains can be places of revelation. Many encounters between God and his people take place on mountains: Abraham, Moses, and Elijah are good Old Testament examples, and from the New Testament we have Christ preaching the Sermon on the Mount, the mount of the Transfiguration (plate 8) and the hill of Golgotha. It is not surprising, therefore, that the background to the Nativity should be shown as mountainous.

A sacred task

Iconographers must be familiar with the language of icons, and with the materials they use - the timber for the board, the gesso, the pigments, and the egg tempera used to paint or write the icon. The wisdom and skills handed down from others enable them to take their place in this sacred tradition. Their spiritual and artistic discipline belong together as a preparation for being servants of God for this particular work. The life of prayer and fidelity to the Faith and the Sacraments are the foundation from which creative work develops. The task is to bring into being an icon which will open up for others something of the mystery of Christ, whether the image is of Christ himself, his Mother, the Saints or events in the life of Christ. This is a sacred task in which the iconographer is the servant, not the master, and in which he or she needs to be profoundly familiar with the tradition.

As we explore this tradition we come to appreciate the truth of what was affirmed by St Theodore of Studium in the 9th century, "Hearing is equal to sight and it is necessary to use both senses". Religious and spiritual language is visual as well as verbal. This is clearly stated in the *Catechism of the Catholic Church*: "Christian iconography expresses in images the same Gospel message that Scripture communicates by words. Image and word illuminate each other".

What do we discover through the Holy Icons?

The New Testament presents us with the Good News of Jesus Christ, the Son of God, the Saviour of the world in narrative form in the Gospels of Matthew, Mark and Luke. In St John's Gospel we have a series of episodes which are crystallized around images such as the Temple of God, the Light of the World, the Good Shepherd, the Bread of Life and the True Vine. The climax of these is the passion, death and resurrection of Jesus, and St John says that all this has been "written that you may believe that Jesus is the Christ, the Son of God, and that believing you may have life in his name" (*Jn* 20:31). The point of presenting the story is that we may have life in Christ. The New Testament is witness to the faith that something dramatic has changed the whole nature of human life: new possibilities have appeared; God has entered into human life so that we might enter into the divine life. We have been raised with Christ. Already in this life we share the life of heaven, the life of the world to come.

I suggest that the following texts from St John and the letters to the Ephesians and the Colossians should form a sort of springboard from which to approach the holy icons. The icons express in visual form what the New Testament expresses in words. It is about "Life in His Name", the life of the baptized - not a past experience, but a present reality made possible by the historical events of the Incarnation. So look at *Jn* 1:14, 16-18; 10:10; 12:46. *Ep* 1:3,7-10 and *Col* 1:13-14, 21-22, 27; 2:1-3, 9-10, 13; 3:1-4. You will notice some 'big' words such as grace, truth, light, spiritual blessings, the heavenly places, forgiveness, redemption, wisdom, understanding, knowledge, insight, mystery, glory, treasures, fullness, kingdom, beloved Son. But there are also 'little' words that we easily overlook, such as in, with, through. These act as connectors which define how we relate to the 'big' words: *in* the bosom of the Father, *in* darkness, *in* the heavenly places, *in* all wisdom, *in* him; together *with* him, *with* Christ, *with* Christ *in* God; *through* Moses, *through* Jesus Christ. We are placed in specific relationships, with Christ in God, beholding the glory of the Incarnate Son, raised with Christ, already enjoying the spiritual blessings of the heavenly places, already living in the light of grace and truth, and awaiting the final entrance into glory.

Doors to another world

Earlier I said, "Click on the icon and you enter a whole new world of information and imagery". With the holy icons we do rather more than just "click" on them: we enter more deeply into those relationships expressed in the last paragraph. It is not surprising that the holy icons are often referred to as doors or windows: something through which we pass to another place, or through which we look into another world. These are appropriate terms, for with icons we are not looking at images of dead people, or dead historical events. We are not looking at scenes which would be better expressed through photography. The holy icons present us with persons and events seen in the light of the transfiguring and redeeming grace of God; they take us up into the light of God's eternity, grace and truth, and nourish in us the "life in his name" which is manifested through the Incarnation.

In the Apocalypse St John says, "I looked, and lo, in heaven an open door!" (*Rv* 4:1). Through that open door he enters into the heavenly worship and the place of revelation. In C. S. Lewis's *The Lion, the Witch and the Wardrobe*, the children enter the strange world of Narnia through the wardrobe. Human life and literature include many extra-ordinary experiences - changes in levels of consciousness and perception which can only be communicated through the metaphors and imagery of transition. Sacred iconography uses its own language of symbols and imagery to take us deeper into the mystery of Christ.

In the late 10th century the Russian Prince Vladimir sent emissaries to find out about Christianity in various parts of Europe. Their experience of worship in the Cathedral of Haghia Sophia in Constantinople led to the conversion of the Prince and his people. The *Russian Primary Chronicle* reports the reactions of the emissaries: "We knew not whether we were in heaven or on earth, for surely there is no such splendour or beauty anywhere upon earth. We cannot describe it to you: only this we know, that God dwells there among men, and that their service surpasses the worship of all other places. For we cannot forget that beauty." Beauty, and the union of heaven and earth remain key elements in the Orthodox tradition of worship; both are expressed through the holy icons.

Where do we see the Holy Icons?

For over 70 years many books have been published about icons, from many standpoints. Most people who are interested in icons have probably seen more icons in books than they have 'in the flesh'. Travel to the countries of Eastern Europe, Greece, Russia and the Holy Land has given many people a taste for the 'real thing', which is quite different from looking at books and postcards. By far the greatest number of icons have been created within the Orthodox Churches. They are also prominent in Eastern Rite Catholic Churches, and some Western Rite Catholic Churches and communities. To grasp the significance of icons we need to consider them in the context for which they were created: the worship and devotional life of Christians. Within the East Christian tradition icons have a place in the homes of the faithful, often in the 'icon corner' with a lamp burning in front of them. They are focal points for family devotion, and visible signs of the presence of Christ and the saints. The domestic presence of icons brings together the liturgy of the Church and of the home. Three aspects of the iconography of Orthodox churches need to be considered.

The *iconostasis*

First, the *iconostasis* or icon screen, which marks the
division between the altar area and the nave, and
symbolizes the relationship of heaven and earth, the
invisible and the visible worlds. Churches built from the
4th century often had a low barrier or *templon* to mark
this division; later, columns and a beam linking the outer
walls of the sanctuary were added. As early as the 6th
century the beam of the templon was decorated with
icons of Christ and the saints; by the 10th - 11th centuries
the *Deesis* (see p. 41) was becoming a common feature;
from the 12th century onwards the spaces between the
columns began to be filled with icons. In Russia the
upward development of the iconostasis from the 15th
century onwards almost totally obscured the sanctuary.
The design of an iconostasis depends on the size of the
church building. A wide sanctuary gives scope for a large
iconostasis, with the *royal doors* in the centre, a northern
door into the *Prothesis* (where the bread and wine are
prepared for the Divine Liturgy), and a southern door into
the *Diakonikon* (where items used in the liturgy are kept).
There are usually icons of the Annunciation (cf. plate 2),
the four Evangelists, St Basil and St John Chrysostom on
or adjacent to the royal doors; south of these doors there
is an icon of Christ, and to the north an icon of the
Mother of God. Other icons commemorate persons, feasts

or events relating to the dedication of the church. The outer doors usually have icons of the archangels or Deacon saints. Above the royal doors there may be an icon of the Last Supper. Lamps or candles are lit in front of the icons.

The upper extent of the iconostasis depends on the scale of the building and the financial resources available. The *Deesis* tier is centred on an image of Christ in majesty; the Mother of God and St John the Baptist are on either side of Christ, with the archangels Michael and Gabriel, the apostles Peter and Paul, and more saints according to the space available. All the figures assembled on either side of Christ are turned towards him with their hands raised in a gesture of intercession (*deesis* in Greek); their concentrated attentiveness creates a powerful expression of the prayer of the Church in heaven and on earth, united in intercession and adoration. The Church Feasts tier has icons for the major festivals of the liturgical year. At a higher level we may find the tier of icons of the Prophets (including the kings David and Solomon, and Zechariah the father of John the Baptist), all turned towards the image of the Mother of God of the Sign in the centre (cf. plate 6). This central icon represents the fulfilment of Isaiah's prophecy that "the Virgin shall conceive and bear a Son, and shall call him Emmanuel" (*Is* 7:10-14). The icon of the Prophet Isaiah is frequently omitted from this tier, as the fulfilment of his prophecy takes precedence over the prophet himself. At a still higher level there may be the tier of icons of the Old Testament Patriarchs who foreshadow the Christian Church and the New Covenant, and in the centre an icon of the Hospitality of Abraham, with the three angels who prefigure the full revelation of the Holy Trinity through the Incarnation and Pentecost (cf. plate 11).

Our description of the iconostasis began with the Royal Doors, and worked up to the level of the Patriarchs, but theologically it helps to 'read' the iconostasis from the top downwards: from the early stages of salvation and revelation, through the Prophets to the Incarnate life of Christ as celebrated in the Church Feasts. Then we come to our liturgical life in Christ with the *Deesis* group and the other icons at the lowest level. Those who are unfamiliar with the iconostasis often regard it as a barrier between the nave and the sanctuary. This misunderstanding is addressed by the Russian theologian Fr Pavel Florenskii: "The iconostasis conceals nothing from the faithful: it bears witness of the mystery; it discloses to them, the lame and the halt, the entrance to the other world. ... The material iconostasis does not replace the living witness, but testifies to them only, in order to sharpen the spiritual attention of those who pray - for the direction of attention is the indispensable condition for the development of spiritual vision".

Architectural icons

Second, the domes, vaults and walls of domed Orthodox churches are adorned with frescoes and icons, and here we find another pattern of descending images. The interior of the central dome will usually have a figure of Christ Pantocrator, the All-ruling Christ, the sovereign of the universe. His right hand is raised in blessing, while his left hand holds a book or scroll signifying the revelation he gives to the world. The drum beneath the dome will be decorated with images of angels and prophets. In the four pendentives where the drum beneath of the dome joins the vaults of the roof we find the four Evangelists, often shown writing their Gospels. The vaults of the church may have more Church Feasts images, while the walls show saints and martyrs whose witness is an encouragement to the faithful. Revelation comes from above, and within this descending pattern of images and revelation the Church is enfolded. Within that framework she offers her worship.

Icon of the feast-day

Third, in front of the iconostasis there is usually at least one icon on a lectern to be venerated by the faithful when they come into the church. The faithful touch the ground with their right hand and make the sign of the Cross three times, kiss the icon, and again touch the ground and three times make the sign of the Cross. The icon on the stand will be associated with a particular day or season, or the dedication of the Church. In the act of veneration, the icon is kissed as an act of devotion to the person depicted in the icon; through the physical veneration the prototype is honoured.

Seeing Icons

Very few churches outside the Orthodox and Eastern Rite Catholic traditions will have the full iconographical scheme which developed in the Byzantine and Russian traditions. In the Holy Land, the Church of the Multiplication of the Loaves and Fishes at Tabgha has two large panel icons of Christ and the Mother of God at the entrance into the Sanctuary, and St Peter in Gallicantu in Jerusalem has a major series of images relating to the life of St Peter. The most ancient icons can be seen in some churches in Rome, and at St Katherine's Monastery at the foot of Mount Sinai. The monastery at Chevetogne in Belgium combines Eastern and Western Catholic liturgical traditions, and has fully decorated chapels. Major collections of icons can be seen at the Tretyakov Gallery in Moscow, the Russian Museum in St Petersburg and museums of other Russian cities; in the Byzantine and Benaki Museums in Athens, in Ohrid in Macedonia, in Nicosia in Cyprus and at the Scuola di San Nicolo dei Greci in Venice. In the British Isles there are no large public collections of icons; however, small collections can be seen in the British Museum, the Blackburn Museum and Art Gallery, and the National Gallery of Ireland in Dublin. In recent years there have been major exhibitions at the Royal Academy, the Victoria and Albert Museum, the Courtauld Institute and at the Hellenic Centre in London. The Temple Gallery in London has specialized in icons for over 40 years and is always worth a visit. Many Orthodox Christians are distressed to see icons taken out of their liturgical context and displayed as art objects in museums. On the other hand, many people comment on the intensely spiritual atmosphere experienced at the major exhibitions of icons.

Commentary on Plates

1. Portrait of a Bearded Young Man

*(Egypt; Fayyum (?); 2nd Century.
The Temple Gallery, London.)*

This is an example of the panel portraits mentioned on page 14 which were used in Egyptian burial practices during the first four centuries of the Christian era. Archimandrite Vasileios, the Abbot of Iviron Monastery on Mount Athos comments that these portraits "do not highlight the corruptible and transient, but memorialize the eternal and unending." They "represent and manifest that invisible secret which is the soul of man". "A sense of presence is created." "... the people who painted the Fayyum portraits form one unbroken lineage with those who later painted the icons of the Church, where man's salvation is understood and experienced as a release from the ugliness of the passions and a mingling with the divine beauty." (*The Fayyum Portraits*, Alexander Press, Montreal)

2. The Annunciation

(Russian, 16th century. The Temple Gallery, London)

This icon is formed from the upper sections of the two Royal Doors at the centre of an iconostasis. On the left Gabriel holds a staff in his left hand, and extends his right hand in greeting as he appears before the Virgin. On the right, at the top we see a segment of a circle representing the divine realm, with three rays of light shining into the rest of the panel. The Mother of God is seated on a stool with cushions and a raised footrest. She is placed higher than the Archangel, indicating her high level of spiritual maturity, and the humility of Gabriel in his approach to her. Details from the *Protevangelion* or Apocryphal *Book of James* (a late second century work originating in Egypt) have influenced the depiction of the Virgin in icons of the Annunciation; we read there that Mary was allotted the task of preparing the scarlet and purple material to be used in making a veil for the Temple in Jerusalem; the Virgin is shown holding the yarn in one hand, while it falls from the other hand as she is surprised by the appearance of Gabriel. The background to the two figures is an extravagant, surreal architectural composition. We seem to be looking down on the buildings on the left, at Gabriel from our own level, and up to the Virgin. The background setting provides an enclosure for the event in which we contemplate the interaction between Gabriel and Mary, not simply as a past event, but as an encounter which encourages each of us to echo Our Lady's words, "Be it done unto me according to thy word."

The icon is vibrant with joy at this beginning of our salvation. The Orthodox texts for the feast reiterate this, and draw upon symbols from the Old Testament to reveal the fulfilment of God's plan of salvation. "O marvel! God is come among men; he who cannot be contained is contained in a womb; the Timeless enters time; and, strange wonder! his conception is without seed, his emptying is past telling: so great is this mystery! For God empties himself, takes flesh, and is fashioned as a creature, when the angel tells the pure Virgin of her conception: 'Hail, thou who art full of grace: the Lord who has great mercy is with thee'." (FM p. 443 - 444) "Hail O Theotokos, deliverance from the curse of Adam. Hail, holy Mother of God; hail, living Bush. Hail, Lamp; hail, Throne; hail, Ladder and Gate. Hail, divine Chariot; hail, swift Cloud. Hail Temple; hail, Vessel of gold. Hail, Mountain; hail, Tabernacle and Table. Hail, thou release of Eve." (FM p. 459) (cf *Gn* 3:15-17; *Ex* 3:4, 25. 31, *Gn* 28:12,17, *Ezk* 44:2, *Is* 19:1, *Ex* 16:33, *Dt* 2:34-35, *Ex* 26:1, 25.23). These Royal Doors form the centre of an iconostasis; through them the priests and other ministers enter and leave the sanctuary. It is the threshold between the nave (symbolic of the Church's presence on earth)

and the sanctuary (symbolic of the Church in heaven). It is here that the Beatitudes (*Mt* 5:3-12) are read early in the Divine Liturgy. Each of the Beatitudes implies an inversion of our normal human values. The life of the Kingdom of God involves conversion and a transformation of our way of life. The presence of the incarnate Son in the womb of the Virgin is a unique act of divine humility and condescension, but it opens up the way for Christ to dwell in us, together with the Father and the Holy Spirit (cf. *Jn* 14:18-26); it makes possible the presence of the Kingdom in our lives. The Annunciation icon invites us to welcome Christ and the Kingdom of God as gifts which will transform and transfigure our lives. The Mother of God is the supreme example of the welcoming of what God most wants to bestow upon his creation. It is in response to comments about her that Christ says, "Blessed ... are those who hear the word of God and keep it!" (*Lk* 11:28).

3. The Nativity of Christ

(Russian, 15th century.
Gallery di Palazzo Leoni Montanari, Vicenza)

At the upper edge of this icon the dark segment of circle
signifies the divine realm; from it descends a ray of light
which divides into three at the circle with the cruciform
star. Three rays descend into the darkness of the cave. The
dark cave is the place where according to tradition our
Lord was born. Wrapped in white swaddling cloths and
with a white halo the Christ-child lays in the manger,
which looks very much like a sarcophagus or coffin and is
also reminiscent of an altar. The icon brings together
themes of life and death, light and darkness. The ox and
ass indicate the text from Isaiah, "The ox knows its owner,
and the ass its master's crib; but Israel does not know, my
people does not understand" (1:3). The Virgin rests on a
bed and is turned towards the bottom left corner where
Joseph is being tempted to unbelief by the devil disguised
as a shepherd. In the opposite corner the midwives
prepare to bathe the infant Jesus. In the upper section two
angels on the left glorify God, their hands and faces raised
to heaven; a third angel bends down in adoration towards
the Child in the manger. To the right of the Virgin a
shepherd with his sheep blows his trumpet to glorify God.
To the left of the Virgin three Magi approach the cave

bearing gifts. The whole scene is radiant with light, the rocky surface of the mountain reflecting the light. This feast is a celebration of re-creation, the work of God's grace, the Master coming to dwell with his people. The three levels of the icon - the heavenly realm and the angels, the central scene in and around the cave, and the lower section with Joseph and the midwives - are distinct but not absolutely separated. There is descending and ascending movement in the upper two sections: the divine light descends into the cave and an angel bows towards the cave; the gestures of the upper angels towards heaven are echoed in the movement of the Magi towards the Incarnate Son. The gaze of the Virgin takes us down to the lowest level where the figures on the left epitomize doubt and temptation; on the right the activity of the midwives is suggestive of the beginning of our sacramental life in the waters of Baptism. In and through this icon we are lifted up in worship and adoration; our attention moves around within the icon, but always comes back to the central mystery of the Incarnation. The Orthodox texts for the feast illustrate the close relationship between the icon and the liturgical texts, and help us to relish the glory of the Life into which we have been raised in Christ. "The holy sayings of the Prophets (*Is* 7:14, *Mi* 5:2) have been fulfilled in the city of Bethlehem within a cave. The whole creation is made rich: let it rejoice and be of good cheer. The Master of all has come to live with his servants, and from the bondage of the enemy he delivers us who were made subject to corruption (*Rm* 8: 20-21). In swaddling clothes and lying in a manger, he is made manifest a young Child, the pre-eternal God" (FM p. 214). "What shall we offer Thee, O Christ, who for our sakes hast appeared on earth as man? Every creature made by thee offers thee thanks. The angels offer thee a hymn; the heavens a star; the Magi, gifts; the shepherds, their wonder; the earth, its cave; the wilderness, the manger: and we offer thee a Virgin Mother. O pre-eternal God, have mercy upon us" (FM p. 254). "[The Magi] ...saw thee wrapped in swaddling clothes, within a poor and lowly cave, ...and in joy they gazed upon thee, who art at once both man and Lord" (FM p. 270).

4. The Mother of God, *Hodegitria*

(Russian, Moscow c. 1500.
The Temple Gallery, London)

The Hodegon Monastery in Constantinople took its name
from the monks who guided blind pilgrims to a
miraculous spring where sight could be restored.
Hodegon means guide or conductor, and the chief icon of
the Mother of God in the monastery became known as the
Hodegitria: 'She who points the Way'. This image is
known to have existed in the mid-ninth century, but there
are earlier prototypes, and tradition roots its origin in the
work of St Luke. Over the centuries many variants on the
original Byzantine type came into existence. Russian
examples such as this one tend to be less formal and
imbued with a greater tenderness than the Byzantine
images. Abbreviated inscriptions identify the Mother of
God and Jesus Christ; in Our Lord's halo there would
have been cruciform marking and the abbreviation
identifying him as "The One", truly God (cf. plate 7).

With a powerful gesture of the right hand the Mother
of God points to the Son of God who sits enthroned on
her left arm. Christ is shown with a white under-garment
and a rich red outer garment; he has an enlarged forehead
symbolizing his divine wisdom (St Paul is depicted in a
similar way), and holds the scroll indicating the wisdom

he brings to the world; his right hand is raised in blessing. Christ faces us, but his eyes look beyond us. The Mother of God is clothed in a rich red-brown maphorion, beneath which we can see a small part of the blue scarf covering her hair. The three stars may have originated as pins to hold the maphorion, but they came to be regarded as symbols of the perpetual virginity of the Mother of God, before, during and after childbirth. Her hands are visible and prominent, supporting her Son and guiding our attention towards him. The length of thumb and fingers of her right hand stresses their spiritual function - to lead us to Christ. Her posture is turned slightly towards Christ, and her gaze shows contemplative attentiveness in keeping with St Luke's comment that she "kept all these things, pondering them in her heart" (*Lk* 2:19, 51). Her gaze seems to direct us to the spiritual truths and realities that are embodied in her Son, gently reinforcing the gesture of her right hand. Just being present with this icon can evoke a sense of prayer and wonder. There seem to be three 'centres' within this icon: first, the head of the Virgin, second, the head of Christ, and third, the space between the hands of Mother and Son. We can see this mysterious space and the relationship of the hands as the gathering up of our intentions, devotions and intercessions into the prayer of the Mother of God: she offers; he blesses.

5. The icon of the Mother of God, *Eleousa*

(Russian, 16th century. Beuron Archabbey, Germany)

Eleousa - loving-kindness - the Greek word sums up this type of icon in which there is great tenderness and intimacy between Mother and Son. Tradition roots this type in the work of St Luke, but it may well have emerged in Coptic art of the 5th - 6th centuries. Examples of this type are known from the 9th century onwards, the most famous being the *Vladimir Mother of God*, which was created in Constantinople about 1130 and given to the Russian Church, first centred in Kiev, then later in Vladimir and Moscow. The Vladimir Mother of God is deeply associated with Russian history, faith and suffering, and has inspired many copies. While the origins of this type are rooted in the history of Eastern Christianity, developments in the 12th century deepened the intensity of what is expressed in this image. In this period there was an increased interest in the place of the Mother of God in the story of Christ's Passion. Mary's hearing Simeon's words, "A sword will pierce through your own soul also" (*Lk* 2:35) is balanced in the Gospel narrative by her standing at the foot of the Cross as her Son is put to death (*Jn* 19:25). Liturgical texts from this period explore the mystery of Our Lady's part in the suffering of Christ, and these in turn influenced the

iconography. In the Eleousa icons the Passion and Cross of Christ are an unobtrusive but significant presence. "'In my arms I hold Thee a corpse, O loving Lord, who hast brought the dead to life; grievously is my heart wounded and I long to die with Thee', said the All-Pure, 'for I cannot bear to look upon Thee lifeless and without breath'." "Seeing her own Lamb led to the slaughter, Mary His Mother followed Him with the other women and in her grief she cried: 'Where dost Thou go, my child? Why dost Thou run so swiftly? Is there another wedding in Cana, and art Thou hastening there, to turn the water into wine? Shall I go with Thee, my Child, or shall I wait for Thee? O speak some word to me, O Word; do not pass me by in silence'." (LT p. 618 - 620)

The Virgin is enfolded in the red-brown maphorion, and holds her Son in a very protective way; her face is sorrowful, and her eyes look up into the distance, as if contemplating the awesome sacrifice which will be made by her Son and the suffering they will each have to endure. Christ's halo is marked with the Cross; his left hand holds the scroll, but his whole attention is focused on his Mother: his face is turned towards her, his eyes look intensely at her, and with his right hand he touches her chin. There is a primitive simplicity about this icon, and the face of Christ has something of the wide-eyed intensity one sees in Coptic icons. Henri Nouwen speaks of "the compassionate solidarity out of which healing comes forth". It is a good phrase to bear in mind when praying with an icon like this which turns our attention to the compassionate solidarity of God and Man in Christ from whence comes forth forgiveness and healing for the human heart.

6. The Mother of God of the Sign

(Russian, early 17th century. The Temple Gallery, London)

This third type of icon of the Mother of God has its own distinctive form. It is a development of the *Orant* figure which was common in early Christian art, the Virgin is depicted as a personification of prayer and the presence of Christ-Emmanuel on her breast links this image to the prophecy of Isaiah, "Behold, a virgin shall conceive and bear a son, and shall call his name Emmanuel" (*Is* 9:14; cf. *Mt* 1:23). She is the *Theotokos*, the God-bearer. This icon is intimately linked with the Incarnation. The God whom nothing can contain is contained within the womb of the Virgin in order that he may accomplish our salvation. The enlarged forehead and the scroll indicate Christ's wisdom, and his right hand is raised in blessing. The mandorla within which Christ is represented is placed within the chalice-shaped form of the raised arms of the Virgin and the embroidered lower edge of her garment. The whole of the image is in turn contained within the tabernacle of the icon itself. The restrained form of the icon, and the faces of the Virgin and her Son looking directly out from the icon invite us to become *Orant* people, and God bearers. We are to raise our hands in prayer in order to receive the fullness of grace and goodness which God wishes to bestow upon us. The place of this icon in the iconostasis has been mentioned on page 41.

7. Christ the Saviour

(Russian, Moscow School; first quarter of 16th Century.
Rublyov Museum of Old Russian Art, Moscow)

This icon is in the long tradition of head and torso images with the halo extending into the upper section of the border. There is great calmness and stability in the figure of Christ on a gold background. The inner and outer garments of the Saviour are clearly distinguished; from within the outer garment his right hand is directed towards his heart, the centre of his being, the source of his love and goodness; his left hand holds the book, externalizing the inner wisdom, discernment and knowledge that is present in Christ. His face is central to the upper section of the icon, and calmly embraces us within his gaze; his right hand invites us to come to him, and many icons of this kind have the text, "Come to me, all who labour and are heavy laden, and I will give you rest. Take my yoke upon you, and learn from me; for I am gentle and lowly in heart, and you will find rest for your souls. For my yoke is easy, and my burden is light." (*Mt* 11:28-30). Here, however, the text is: "Do not judge by appearances, but judge with right judgement" (*Jn* 7:24). "Judge not , that you be not judged. For with the judgement you pronounce you will be judged, and the measure you give will be the measure you get" (Mt 7:1-2). The face of Christ and the text of the book address us directly.

8. The Transfiguration of Christ

(Greek, c 1500. The Temple Gallery, London)

The theme of Christ's glory permeates the whole of St John's Gospel, echoing the words in the Prologue: "We have beheld his glory, glory as of the only Son from the Father" (*Jn* 1:14). In the synoptic Gospels the Transfiguration is the key episode when Christ's glory is perceived by Peter, James and John. (Cf. *Mt* 17:1-8; *Mk* 9:2-8; *Lk* 9:28-36.) Just as St John sees the Passion and Cross as Christ's glorification (*Jn* 13:31), so do the other evangelists see a connection between the Transfiguration and the Cross. All this is wonderfully summed up in a text for the feast: "Thou wast transfigured upon the mountain, and thy disciples beheld thy glory, O Christ our God, as far as they were able to do so: that when they saw thee crucified, they might know that thy suffering was voluntary, and might proclaim unto the world that thou art truly the Brightness of the Father." (FM p.489; cf. *Heb* 1:3)

In this icon Christ, Moses and Elijah are placed on separate mountain peaks. Christ is in dazzling white garments, his right hand raised in blessing, and his left hand holding the scroll. Behind Christ a lozenge-shaped mandorla radiates beams of light, and triple-ray flashes of light come down towards the three astounded

disciples, Peter, John and James. The latter two bow down in awe; Peter turns to the Lord: "Master, it is well that we are here; let us make three booths, one for you and one for Moses, and one for Elijah" (*Mk* 9:5). According to Luke, Moses and Elijah "appeared in glory and spoke of his departure, which he was to accomplish at Jerusalem" (*Lk* 9:31).

In this "mountain-top experience" the divine light and the uncreated divine energies are manifested, and as the bright cloud overshadows the disciples, the voice of the Father proclaims the identity of his Son: "This is my beloved Son; listen to him" (*Mk* 9:7). This icon helps us to place ourselves before the beloved Son, sharing in the awe and wonder of three disciples who were later to be with Christ in the garden of Gethsemane. "He revealed his glory to his disciples to strengthen them for the scandal of the Cross. His glory shone from a body like our own, to show that the Church, which is the body of Christ, would one day share his glory" (Preface for the Mass of the Transfiguration in the Roman Rite). The theme of Transfiguration is particularly significant for iconographers, for it is their task to show humanity transfigured and restored to the divine image and likeness in Christ.

9. Anastasis - Resurrection
(Kariye Djami, Istanbul, c. 1315-21)

The earliest surviving example of the image known simply as *The Anastasis* is from the early 8th century. It shows Christ raising Adam and Eve from Hades, and taking them up into glory. This is the central reality of the Resurrection faith: Christ's victory over sin and death, and the raising of humanity to share in the divine life. Christ is raised, and we are raised with him. Our illustration is the fresco in the former monastic church of the Saviour in Chora in Istanbul. The conch of the apse is filled with the scene of Christ trampling down the gates of Hades and shattering the bolts and locks; Adam and Eve are rescued from their tombs. On the left behind Adam stand David and Solomon, Christ's royal and prophetic ancestors, together with John the Baptist and other Old Testament people. On the right behind Eve the group includes Abel, the shepherd son of Adam and Eve who suffered a violent death, and still more Old Testament characters. It is clear that the righteous ones of the Old Covenant are included within Christ's work of redemption. The background to the outer groups of figures is reminiscent of the Exodus story: the earth is rent assunder and raised up like the waters of the Red Sea to allow Christ to lead redeemed humanity out from Hades into the Promised Land of the Kingdom of God.

The figure of Christ is central to the whole composition. He is clothed in radiant white garments, and stands above the open abyss of the underworld against the background of a lozenge-shaped mandorla signifying his divinity. The following quotations show how closely the iconography is linked to the Liturgy. "Christ is risen from the dead, trampling down Death by death, and upon those in the tomb bestowing life." (H p. 226) "Now are all things filled with light; heaven, and earth, and the places under the earth. All Creation doth celebrate the Resurrection of Christ, on whom also it is founded." (H p. 228) "The gates of Death have opened unto Thee in fear, O Lord, and the doorkeepers of Hades quaked when they saw Thee. For Thou hast shattered the gates of brass and smitten the bars of iron in sunder. Thou hast led us out of darkness and the shadow of death, and broken our bonds." (HWE p.287) The final quotation is attributed to St Makarios of Egypt: "When you hear that Christ descended into hell in order to deliver the souls dwelling there, do not think that what happens now is very different. The heart is a tomb and there our thoughts and our intellect are buried, imprisoned in heavy darkness. And so Christ comes to the souls in hell that call upon Him, descending, that is to say, into the depths of the heart; and there he commands death to release the imprisoned souls that call upon Him, for He has power to deliver us. Then, lifting up the heavy stone that oppresses the soul, and opening the tomb, He resurrects us - for we were truly dead - and releases our imprisoned soul from its lightless prison. ... What was the purpose of His descent to earth except to save sinners, to bring light to those in darkness and life to the dead?" (*Phil*. III, p.337)

10. St Sergius of Radonezh (c.1314-1392)

(Russian, early 17th century.
The Temple Gallery, London)

The contribution of St Sergius to the spiritual and political life of Russia is enormous. He lived when the ever-present threats from Tartars seemed destined to wipe out the Russian principalities and their Orthodox faith. St Sergius encouraged Grand Prince Dmitri of Moscow to resist the foreign invaders and drive them out: "Advance without fear, my Lord. Dare to meet their ferocity, and do not fear, for God will assist you". The terrible Battle of Kulikovo Pole (1380) gave substance to the hope that the perennial invaders could be conquered. Eventually Moscow became the centre around which the new Russian state developed. The political influence of St Sergius is remarkable, as his vocation was essentially that of a hermit. He had gone with his brother to live in the forest, but the severity of the conditions led his brother to return to the world. Sergius persevered, and survived the bitter Russian winters. He built a small church dedicated to the Holy Trinity, and this became the heart of his eremitical life. His solitary life of prayer was disturbed by the advent of others who wished to join him, and many communities developed through him. His initial foundation where he is buried continues to be a thriving monastery and place of pilgrimage.

The spirituality of St Sergius was centred on devotion to the Holy Trinity. The significance of this devotion can be summed up in two quotations, the first from his disciple and author of his *Life*, Epiphanius, the second from Fr Pavel Florenskii. "St Sergius built the church of the Holy Trinity as a mirror for his community, that through gazing at the divine Unity they might overcome the hateful divisions of the world." "St Sergius understood the azure blue of the heavens [as the emblem] of the imperturbable world of eternal and perfect love. He understood that world of love as both the object of contemplation and the commandment to be realized in every life - as the foundation for the building of the Church and the person, of government, of society." Some time after Sergius's death abbot Nikon asked one of the saint's disciples, Andrei Rublev, to paint an icon which would express the fundamental nature of the Trinitarian revelation which was at the heart of Sergius's faith and devotion. This was probably completed in either 1411 or 1425-27, and is the subject of the next section.

This image of St Sergius is a half-length figure set centrally within the tabernacle of the icon, facing us; the large forehead and the scroll indicate his great wisdom. His outer garment covers the monastic habit whose cruciform decoration is visible where the cloak is separated by the hands. The raised right hand is turned inward, to the heart, as if indicating the 'prayer of the heart' which is the foundation of Orthodox monastic prayer. The white highlights on the head, face, beard and cloak of the saint indicate a transfigured life, a person who is luminous with the divine presence. The great sense of stillness and recollection seems to incarnate the teaching of the spiritual tradition within which St Sergius and his disciples were nurtured.

"Continuity of attention produces inner stability; inner stability produces a natural intensification of watchfulness; and this intensification gradually and in due measure gives contemplative insight into spiritual warfare. This in turn is succeeded by persistence in the Jesus Prayer..." "Extreme watchfulness and the Prayer of Jesus Christ, undistracted by thoughts, are the necessary basis for inner vigilance and unfathomable stillness of soul...This watchfulness and this Prayer must be intense, concentrated and unremitting". (St Hesychios the Priest. ? Sinai; 8th or 9th Cent. *Phil* I, pp.163-4).

11. The Holy Trinity Icon of Andrei Rublev

(Russian, Andrei Rublev c. 1411 or 1425-27.
The Bridgeman Art Library)

Long before Andrei Rublev created this icon, the mysterious event known as the Hospitality of Abraham (*Gn* 18) had been reflected on by Christian theologians and spiritual writers. This event foreshadowed the Trinitarian revelation given through Christ and fulfilled by gift of the Holy Spirit at Pentecost. The event is illustrated in mosaics and icons from the 4th century onwards, often in connection with the Eucharist. This tradition of theology and iconography would have been familiar to St Sergius and to Andrei Rublev. The icon which Rublev created in memory of St Sergius omits the ancillary characters: Abraham, Sarah and the servants have no place in this image. Rublev uses the images of the three angels to take us into the mysterious relationships within the Godhead between the Father, the Son and the Holy Spirit.

The geometric forms within the icon include the circle and the octagon; the circle is a symbol for perfection and divinity; the octagon suggests the glory of the eighth day, the Sabbath rest of the Kingdom of God. Within these two enveloping forms we find the rectangular table at which the angels are seated. A strong sense of axial

symmetry is created with the broad vertical central section moving up from the space between the footstools, to the chalice, the central angel and the tree. The heads of the three angels suggest a horizontal line intersecting with the vertical central line, giving a cruciform structure. The inverse perspective of the seats and footstools focuses on whoever stands before the icon, and also creates divergent lines which take us up into the icon. In the upper section three details carried over from the Hospitality of Abraham have become very stylized. On the left the architectural feature is a 'remnant' of the house of Abraham and Sarah; in the centre, the tree suggests the oak of Mamre, where the mysterious visitation occurred; and on the right the mountain could refer to Mount Moriah, and Abraham's willingness to sacrifice his son Isaac there. There is circular movement within the icon which goes in two directions: anti-clockwise, suggested by the bowed heads of the angels in the centre and on the right, and the form of the mountain and the tree; clockwise, expressed in the way the staffs of the three angels fan out to the right. Within these circular forms and movement the bodies of the outer angels create a form which echoes the shape of the chalice on the table.

On the left the angel signifies the Person of the Father, with translucent, diaphanous robes; the central angel indicates the Person of the Son, whose robes are more substantial, and in both colour and form can be associated with icons of Christ the Saviour; the angel on the right represents the Person of the Holy Spirit, with green robes - the colour associated with the Holy Spirit. The details in the upper section of the icon can now be seen from a different perspective: the mountain gains a more universal significance as a symbol of experience of God; the oak of Mamre can be linked with the Tree of Life in the Garden of Eden and the Holy City (*Gn* 3 and *Rv* 22:1-5), and with the Cross of Christ; the 'remnant' of the house of Abraham and Sarah can now be seen as a symbol of the Father's House, the destiny of our lives, the goal of our journey (*Jn* 14:1-3). In the central space of the table stands a simple chalice with the head of an animal, reminiscent of the calf killed by Abraham for his visitors, the ram caught in the thicket on Mount Moriah, and the Passover Lamb which foreshadows the coming of Christ as the Lamb of God, taking away the sin of the world. The central angel's right hand is stretched out towards the chalice, indicating the willingness of the Son to undertake the sacrificial work of incarnation and redemption; the raised hand of the angel on the right indicates the co-operation of the Holy Spirit in this work of fulfilling the Father's will.

The whole of this icon is suffused with light and colour. Here are no shadows; here is no darkness. Here we see the mystery of self-giving love and mutual in-dwelling. There is a still centre around which movement takes place, a form and content similar to that of the Nativity icon. The Nativity icon shows us the Incarnation by which we are restored to Life. The Trinity icon shows us the Divine Life into which we have been raised up. Appropriate words to conclude this section come from the end of the second Eucharistic Prayer in the Roman Missal: "Have mercy on us all; make us worthy to share eternal life with Mary, the virgin Mother of God, with the apostles, and with all the saints who have done your will throughout the ages. May we praise you in union with them, and give you glory through your Son, Jesus Christ. Through him, with him, in him, in the unity of the Holy Spirit, all glory and honour is yours, almighty Father, for ever and ever, Amen."

Living and Praying with the Holy Icons

We should beware of treating icons as a 'spirituality technique' that may serve us until we move on to something different. For Orthodox Christians and for Eastern-Rite Catholics the holy icons are at the heart of their mainstream Christian experience. To grow up in a Church culture which is imbued with the art of the holy icons gives a distinct dimension to worship and prayer. The icons are a natural part of the spiritual and religious environment, not a fringe 'extra'. From childhood such Christians will light candles in front of icons, kiss them, and make the sign of the Cross in front of them; they will know how to stand, and how make the prostrations that are a bodily aspect of prayer, and will naturally pray with their eyes open. The icons of Christ, the Mother of God and the Saints indicate a presence in the Church every bit as 'real' as the presence of the other people who are present 'in the flesh'. Greeting and venerating the icons is as natural as greeting and welcoming other people in the congregation. For those of us who have not had this background, our 'discovery' of icons is a very different process. We might have been moved by the experience of worship in an Orthodox church, or have seen a particular icon which held our attention. We might have been amazed at the sheer wonder and beauty of icons in an exhibition, entering into a new world of art and religious experience. We are influenced by what we see, and the impact of faith and theology expressed in colour can be very powerful. There may be a strong intuitive element in how we respond to icons. I was moved by an account in Heather Ward's book, *The Gift of Self*, of how she spent most of a week at Taizé doing little else but sitting in front of the Community's icon of the Mother of God, and how this 'being present' before the icon deeply affected her prayer and her sense of vocation. My own first response to the icon in plate 5 was very intuitive, and 40 years later that intuition remains strong.

A place for devotion

Many Orthodox families have an 'icon corner' in their home, with an icon on a small shelf, and a lamp nearby. There may be more than one icon. This corner will be the focal point for individual and family devotion, a normal part of domestic life. In seeking to create an icon corner or similar place of prayer it is best to keep to a small number of icons. The icons should be ones which have a particular significance to us so that they become integrated into our life of prayer, and the place likewise has to be one which actually is conducive to prayer. In a busy household various people may need their own prayer corner away from the rest of the family. The point of having such a place is that it may be *used* for praying.

A wide variety of praying can take place in front of icons, just as all sorts of prayer is offered up from every human heart. If we are praying with eyes open, looking at the icon, the icon itself will prompt and shape our praying. A Mother of God icon could lead us to reflect on the mystery of the Incarnation, the role of Mary, the intimacy which is established between God and his people, the courage and tenderness of Mary, and the way she points us to her Son. We might be moved to intercede for parents and children. Our awareness of other people's pain and suffering might lead us to offer it up to Our Lady, seeking her maternal help and compassion for others. An icon of Christ in majesty can move us to acts of adoration of the Lord for his glory, his goodness and love; we can thank him for the way he calls us to serve him; we can acknowledge him as the Lord of the Universe, the King of Glory, worshipped and adored by saints and angels. Icons of the saints prompt us to reflect on their lives, and to ask for their assistance.

The Prayer corner

The use of a prayer corner is very much in keeping with our Lord's teaching about prayer: "When you pray, go into your room and shut the door and pray to your Father who is in secret; and your Father who sees in secret will reward you" (*Mt* 6:6). It can be a place where we can do the 'work' of prayer, as well as being relaxed and at ease in the presence of God. We can use it for formal prayers, or for the "Prayer of the Church" as we pray the Divine Office. We might also find ourselves in contemplative or affective prayer, being with God, speaking simply and directly to him, or just being silent and still. "Be still and know that I am God" (*Ps* 46:10) is a good text to bear in mind. There is an Orthodox tradition which is summed up in the phrase, "Stand naked before God, with the mind in the heart". We are to stand before God without any pretence, with no "dressing up", no *façade* to hide behind. Having the mind in the heart means being aware of what is going on in the depths of our being. It could be awareness of our sins and failures, of memories good and bad. It could be awareness of the blessings and graces we have received, and a strong sense of God's providential love and care. Jesus said, "Your Father knows what you need before you ask him" (*Mt* 6:8), and that's a good text from which to start praying. He also said, "You are of more value than many sparrows!" (*Mt* 10:31), and that too is worth remembering if we have a depressingly low view of ourselves. Some people find it hard to believe that God does actually love them.

If we use a prayer corner or icon corner regularly it will become 'holy ground', the place where we come before God, a place of meeting. Being in the presence of

Our Lord Jesus Christ changed the lives of his disciples and apostles, and that process of transformation and transfiguration has continued through the ages. In praying with icons we are not simply beholding beautiful works of art; we are being put in touch with the divine beauty and the divine energies which transfigure and re-create us in the image and likeness of God. In giving time to God as we sit, or stand or kneel before the holy icons we place ourselves where we are open to God, without pretence, and by our very presence indicate that there is a desire in our hearts to love the Lord our God with all our heart, and mind, and soul, and strength, and the desire to drink in abundance from the Fountain of Life.

Further reading

Baggley, John, *Doors of Perception - Icons and their spiritual significance* (London, Mowbray; New York, St Vladimir's Seminary Press 1987).

Baggley, John, *Festival Icons for the Christian Year* (London, Mowbray; New York, St Vladimir's Seminary Press, 2000)

Evseyeva, L, and others, translated by Kate Cook, *A History of Icon Painting* (Moscow, "Grand-Holding" Publishers, 2005)

Forest, Jim, *Praying with Icons*, (Orbis)

Onasch, Konrad and Schnieper, Annemarie, Translated by Daniel G. Conklin, *Icons - the Fascination and the Reality* (New York, The Riverside Book Company Inc, 1997

Ouspensky, Leonid and Lossky, Vladimir, *The Meaning of Icons* (New York, St Vladimir's Seminary Press, 1982)

Ramos-Poqui, Guillem, *The Technique of Icon Painting*, (Burns & Oates / Search Press, 1990)

Stuart, John, *Ikons*, (London, Faber and Faber, 1975)

Temple, Richard, *Icons: Divine Beauty* (London, SAQI in association with The Temple Gallery, 2004)

Abbreviations

FM - *The Festal Menaion* translated by Mother Mary and Archimandrite Kallistos Ware. (London & Boston, Faber and Faber 1984)

LT - *The Lenten Triodion* translated by Mother Mary and Archimandrite Kallistos Ware. (London & Boston, Faber and Faber 1984)

H - *Service Book of the Holy Orthodox-Catholic Apostolic (Greco-Russian) Church* compiled and translated by Isabel Florence Hapgood. (Boston & New York, Houghton, Mifflin and Company 1906)

HWE - *The Services for Holy Week and Easter Sunday* from the Triodion and Pentecostarion according to the use of the Orthodox Greek Church in London. (London, Williams & Norgate, 1915)

Phil. - *The Philokalia* translated from the Greek and edited by G. E. H. Palmer, Philip Sherrard and Kallistos Ware, (London & Boston, Faber and Faber; four volumes, 1979, 1981, 1984, 1995)

Acknowledgements

The author is grateful to Stratford Caldecott and Pierpaolo Finaldi for their encouragement in the writing of this booklet. He would also like to express his gratitude to Richard Temple and others who have provided illustrations in the booklet, to Bishop Kallistos Ware for permission to use his translations of Orthodox liturgical texts, and to friends who have made valuable comments and suggestions about the text and overall content of the booklet.

Picture credits

p. 46, 50-51, 58, 65, 69, 77 courtesy of the Temple Gallery London. p. 61 courtesy of Beuron Abbey Germany. p. 67 Russian, Moscow School; first quarter of 16th Century. Rublyov Museum of Old Russian Art, Moscow. p. 54 Natale di Cristo Novgorod c. 1475 tempera on wood, 58,5 x 43,6 cm © Collezione Intesa, Vicenza, Gallerie di Palazzo Leoni Montanari. Cover and p. 72-73 The Anastasis Kariye Djami, Istanbul, c. 1315-21 © Pierpaolo Finaldi. p. 80 The Holy Trinity Icon of Andrei Rublev, (Russian, Andrei Rublev c. 1411 or 1425-27. The Bridgeman Art Library).